Stralsund

Harry Hardenberg

Stralsund

Der Bildband für die Hosentasche
The pocket-sized coffee-table book

steffen verlag

4 | Die Stralsunder Altstadt – Blick vom Turm der Marienkirche

The old city of Stralsund – view from the tower of St. Mary's Church | 5

6 | Ensemble norddeutscher Backsteingotik: St.Nikolai und Rathaus

Einkaufsmeile Ossenreyerstraße
Ossenreyerstrasse – the shopping mile

◄ Trubel in der Ossenreyerstraße
Bustling Ossenreyerstrasse

Winterstimmung
Winter atmosphere

◄ Stadtmauer
City wall

14 | Der Alte Markt – die gute Stube der Stadt

Das jährliche historische Stadtfest für Groß und Klein
The annual historical city festival for old and young

◄ Die Wallensteintage erinnern an den Dreißigjährigen Krieg.
The Wallenstein Festival commemorates the Thirty Years' War.

19

Die 1944 zerstörte Fährbrücke wurde 1994 wieder aufgebaut.
The ferry bridge destroyed in 1944 was reconstructed in 1994.

◄ »Seglarträff« – Erinnerung an fast 200 Jahre
schwedische Verwaltung
'Seglarträff' maritime festival – a reminder of
almost 200 years of Swedish administration

24 | Blick vom Ozeaneum auf die Altstadt

The annual Port Festival is an important event. | 27

Im Meeresmuseum im Katharinenkloster, seit 1951 ständig erweitert
The Oceanographic Museum collection in St. Catherine's Abbey,
constantly expanding since 1951

Schattenbild des Rathauses in der tief stehenden Wintersonne
The City Hall's shadow cast by the low winter sun

◄ Heilgeiststraße
Heilgeiststrasse

'Seglarträff' at the harbour – the romance of sailing in a historical setting | 35

Läden im Erdgeschoss des 2001 sanierten Rathauses
Shops in the ground level of the City Hall, renovated in 2001

Innenhof des Rathauses ➤
Inner courtyard of the City Hall

Westportal mit wertvollen barocken Schnitzereien
West portal with precious Baroque carvings

◄ St. Nikolai – eine der am besten ausgestatteten Kirchen Nordeuropas
St. Nicholas' – one of the best endowed churches of Northern Europe   39

Sommerliches »Wasserspiel« auf dem Alten Markt
Summer 'water games' on the Old Market

Rast auf dem Alten Markt ➤
Relaxing in the Old Market

44 | Die neue Rügenbrücke (2007) und der Rügendamm über den Strelasund

The new Rügen Bridge (2007) and the Rügen Causeway across the Strelasund | 45

Das gotische Wulflam-Haus am Alten Markt
The Gothic Wulflam House on the Old Market

Reminiszenz an das Hotel Goldener Löwe: Haus Nr. 1 am Alten Markt ➤
Recalling the Hotel Goldener Löwe (Golden Lion Hotel) at No. 1, Old Market

The Holy Spirit Hospital provided shelter for sick and poor people, C13th. | 49

Schiffsschraube am Hafenamt
Ship's propeller at the port authority

»Allen auf See Gebliebenen ...« – Gedenkstein an der Seestraße ➤
'For all those lost at sea ...' – memorial stone at Seestrasse

Stralsund celebrates its annual Port Festival. | 57

Keramikrelief von Paul Horn am Silo IV.
Ceramic relief by Paul Horn at Silo IV.

Hafenansicht mit den Speichern aus den 1930er Jahren ➤
Harbour view with warehouses from the 1930s

Blick in das Quartier des Heilgeisthospitals
View of the Heilgeist (Holy Spirit) Hospital Quarter

◄ Die Häuser in der Badstüberstraße erzählen vom Mittelalter.
The houses in Badstüberstrasse recount the Middle Ages.

64 | Riesen des Meeres im Ozeaneum auf der nördlichen Hafeninsel

Giants of the sea in the Ozeaneum aquarium at the northern Harbour Island | 65

Die Stralsunder Altstadt– Blick vom Turm der Marienkirche
The old city of Stralsund – View from the tower of St. Mary's Church

◄ **Blick in Richtung Süden**
  View to the south

68 | Tastmodell der Altstadt auf dem Alten Markt, 2005

Stadtwappen im Giebelfeld des Kommandantenhauses, 2003 erneuert
Municipal coat of arms on the Commander's House, rebuilt in 2003

Erinnerung an Schwedenzeit: Kommandantenhaus am Alten Markt, 1750 ►
Reminder of the Swedish era: Commander's House at Old Market, 1750

72 | Marinelazarett – Große Parower Straße (1936–38), heute Hanseklinikum

Naval Hospital (1936–38), today it is the Hanseatic Hospital I 73

74 | Drei-Kirchen-Blick von der Nordmole aus

View of three churches from the northern pier | 75

Bärenrelief über der Tür der Badenstraße 45, rekonstruiert 1985–89
Relief of a bear above the door of Badenstrasse 45, reconstructed in 1985–89

◄ »Dreimädchenbrunnen« von Günter Kaden in der Fährstraße
'Fontain of the Three Girls' by Günter Kaden in Fährstrasse

Giebelhäuser in der Ossenreyerstraße
Gabled houses in Ossenreyerstrasse

In der Mönchstraße ➤
In Mönchstrasse

The Knieper Pond in winter | 81

Kreuzung Ossenreyerstraße/Heilgeiststraße, das neu errichtete Quartier 17
The corner of Ossenreyerstrasse & Heilgeiststrasse, the redeveloped District 17

Ossenreyerstraße 7–5; in Nr. 6 wurde die Malerin E. Büchsel geboren ►
Ossenreyerstrasse 7–5; the artist E. Büchsel was born in No. 6

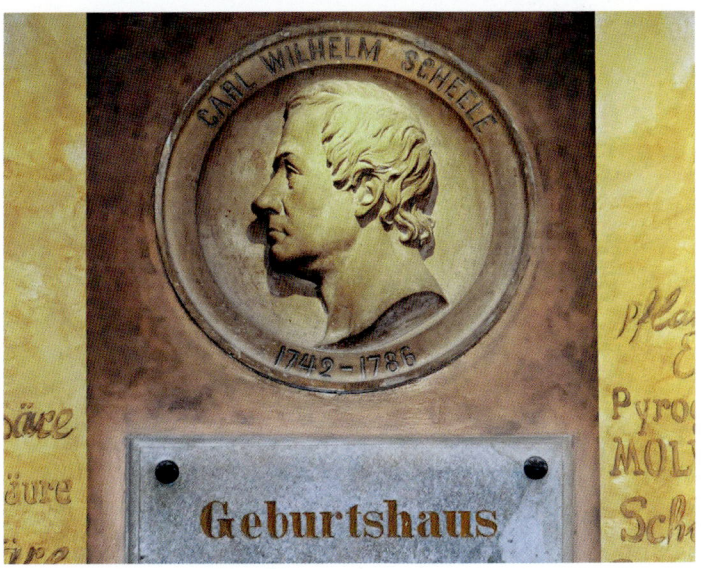

Ein Relief und eine Gedenktafel ehren den Entdecker des Sauerstoffs.
A relief and a plaque commemorate the discoverer of oxygen.

◄ Fährstraße 24 (rotes Haus links): Geburtshaus von Carl Scheele
Fährstrasse 24 (red house on the left): birthplace of Carl Scheele

In the first inner courtyard of St. John's Monastery | 87

Giebelhäuser in der Badenstraße
Gabled houses in Badenstrasse

◄ Ausstellung zum UNESCO-Welterbe Stralsund: Ossenreyerstraße 1
Exhibition for the UNESCO World Heritage site of Stralsund:
Ossenreyerstrasse 1

Der Kampische Hof in der Mühlenstraße
The Kampischer Hof buildings in Mühlenstrasse

◄ Mühlenstraße
Mühlenstrasse

Knieper Pond with the Kütertor gatehouse, St. Nicholas' and St. Catherine's | 93

In der Fährstraße
In Fährstrasse

◄ Bummel durch die Fährstraße
Strolling along Fährstrasse

Idylle im »Arnd Schwarte Gang«
Idyll in the Arnd Schwarte Gang alleyway

98 | Südhafen mit neuer Rügenbrücke und altem Rügendamm

South harbour with new Rügen Bridge and old Rügen Causeway | 99

Kniepertor
Kniepertor gatehouse

Kütertor Innenseite
Kütertor gatehouse inner facade

Kütertor ➤
Kütertor gatehouse

Tribseer Straße
Tribseer Strasse

Milchbar am Neuen Markt ➤
Milk bar on New Market

Proviantmagazin
Provisions storehouse

Wappen der pommerschen Herzöge am Landständehaus, Badenstraße 39
Arms of the Pomeranian dukes at Landstände House, Badenstrasse 39

◄ Kniepertor
Kniepertor gatehouse

St. Nikolai
St. Nicholas' Church

◄ St. Nikolai, Mittelschiff
St. Nicholas' Church nave

St. Nikolai, Predella des Hochaltars: Beschneidung Christi
St. Nicholas' Church: predella of the high altar depicting
the Circumcision of Christ

◄ Backsteingebäude hinter der Nikolaikirche aus dem 14. Jh.
Brick building behind St. Nicholas' Church from the 14th Century

HOSPITALIBVS . SACRIS.
DICATAM . QVONDAM . HANC . AEDEM.
SED . HORRENDO.
PVLVERIS . TORMENTARII . ICTV.
MISERE . DEVASTATAM.
INSTAVRAVIT.
ET . IAM
RECIPIVNDIS SANANDISQVE AEGRIS
SACRAM . ESSE . IVSSIT.
PROVIDA.
AMPLISSIMI . ORDINIS.
PIETAS.

EX . SC . F . FF . AEDILES.
E . H . DE . KANZOW . E . I . SCHVTTE . C . SOHST.

Scheele Apotheke
Scheele Pharmacy

Löwen-Kabinett
Löwen's Cabinet

◄ **Das Stralsund Museum im ehemaligen Katharinenkloster**
Stralsund Museum in the former St. Catherine's Abbey

Heiliger Georg
Saint George

◄ Gedenkstein für den schwedischen Offizier Petersson am Kniepertor
Memorial stone for the Swedish officer Petersson at Kniepertor gate 131

Im Zoo
In the zoo

136 | Zweiter Innenhof des Johannisklosters

Heiliger Paulus
Saint Paul

◄ Apollonienkapelle an der Südseite der Marienkirche, 1416
Chapel of St. Apollonia at the south side of St. Mary's, 1416

Wallensteintage
Wallenstein Festival

Krämergestühl, 1574
Krämer Stalls, 1574

Archivtür, um 1400
Archive door, around 1400

◄ St. Nikolai
St. Nicholas' Church

»Die Hockende« (H.-P. Jaeger) vor der Gaststätte »Ventspils«, Sundpromenade
'The Crouching Woman' (by H.-P. Jaeger) at Ventspils Restaurant, Sund Promenade

Schill-Denkmal von Hans Weddo von Glümer, Sarnowstraße ➤
Schill Memorial by Hans Weddo von Glümer, Sarnowstrasse

148 | Blick von der Nordmole auf den Hafen

Stadtmauer am Knieperwall
City wall along the Knieper Wall

◄ Wiekhäuser am Knieperwall
Guard houses along the Knieper Wall

Hafentage
Port Festival

154

Posaunenengel
Trumpet angel

◄ Barockorgel von Friedrich Stellwagen in St. Marien, 17. Jh.
Baroque organ by Friedrich Stellwagen in St. Mary's, C17th.

157

Kulturkirche St. Jakobi
St. James' Church Cultural Centre

Eröffnung des Ozeaneums am 11. Juli 2008
Opening of the Ozeaneum aquarium on 11th July 2008

Im Ozeaneum: Seeadler ➤
In the Ozeaneum aquarium: sea eagle

Das 1873 fertiggestellte Garnisonslazarett am Neuen Markt
The Garrison Military Hospital completed in 1873 at the New Market

◄ Katharinenberg
Katharinenberg Street

Wintergäste
Winter guests

Gründungsurkunde
Foundation charter

Stadtmauer ►
City wall

Die Alte Stadtwaage in der Wasserstraße
The Old Weighing House in Wasserstrasse

Neubau neben der Alten Stadtwaage ➤
New building besides the Old Weighing House

Das Marinemuseum auf dem Dänholm, Nebenstelle des Stralsund Museums
The Naval Museum at Dänholm island, local branch of the Stralsund Museum

The 'swarm' fish tank in the Ozeaneum aquarium | 183

Hauptraum der Heilgeistkirche
Interior of the Heilgeist Church

◄ Heilgeisthospital und Kirche St. Marien
Holy Spirit Hospital and St. Mary's Church

Panoramic view from the top level of the 'Am Ozeaneum' Car Park | 187

Frühling in Stralsund
Spring in Stralsund

◄ »Arschkerbe« – alter Name für die Gasse zwischen
Franken- und Papenstraße
'Arschkerbe' ('Bum crack') – old name for the lane
between Frankenstrasse and Papenstrasse

In der Kulturkirche
In the Cultural Church

Hafentage
Port Festival

194 | Tradition trifft Moderne – Blick von Altefähr (Rügen)

Zur **Ehre Gottes.**

Ist Dieses Hauß deß H. Geistes

So ANNO 1628. Von der Feinde geschütz gantz ver-
dorben/ Widerumb New erbawet/ ANNO 1647.

Relief am Osttor des Kirchganges
Relief on the eastern gateway of Kirchgang (Church Way)

◄ Relief am Nordgiebel des Elendenhauses des Heilgeisthospitals
Relief on the northern gable of the poorhouse at the Heilgeist
(Holy Spirit) Hospital

Ausstellungseröffnung in der Kulturkirche St. Jakobi
Exhibition opening in the St. James' Church Cultural Centre

Kreuzrippengewölbe im Stralsund Museum
Ribbed vaulting in Stralsund Museum

206 | Das Tunnelaquarium im Ozeaneum

Karl-Liebknecht-Relief von K. Lembke in Knieper West
Karl Liebknecht relief by K. Lembke in the Knieper West district

◄ Ehemals Stasi-Zentrale – heute Studentenquartier, Prohner Straße
Former Stasi headquarters – today a student hall of residence,
Prohner Strasse

»Hiddenseer Goldschmuck« im Stralsund Museum
The Hiddensee Treasure in Stralsund Museum

◄ Barockes Taufgestühl in der Marienkirche
Baroque Baptism Stall in St. Mary's Church

»Seehund« von M. Prerad vor dem Ozeaneum
'Seal' by M. Prerad in the Ozeaneum

◄ Im Ozeaneum
In the Ozeaneum

Altes Handwerk auf den Wallensteintagen im Sommer
Traditional crafts displayed at the Wallenstein Festival in summer

Die »Gorch Fock« in ihrem Heimathafen Stralsund
The ship 'Gorch Fock' in its home port Stralsund

222 | Dem Ozeaneum »aufs Dach gestiegen«

Climbing on the top of the Ozeaneum aquarium | 223

Kanzel in St. Nikolai
Pulpit in St. Nicholas'

225

Fischkutter auf dem Vorhof des Meeresmuseums
Fishing boat in the front yard of the Oceanographic Museum

◄ Vor dem Meeresmuseum
At the Oceanographic Museum

Wappen an der Westseite des Rathauses
Coat of arms on the west side of the City Hall

◄ St. Nikolai und Rathaus – Höhepunkte norddeutscher Backsteingotik
St. Nicholas' Church and City Hall – highlights of North
German Brick Gothic

Traditionssegler »Hanne Marie«
Traditional sailing boat 'Hanne Marie'

Historischer Speicher auf der Hafeninsel ➤
Historical warehouse on the Harbour Island

Sühnestein
Expiatory stone

Zunftzeichen der Gaststätte »Zur Kogge«, Tribseer Straße ►
Guild sign of the restaurant 'Zur Kogge' ('At the Cog'),
Tribseer Strasse

Die Kraweele »Lisa von Lübeck«, von 1999–2004 gebaut
The caravel 'Lisa from Lübeck', built between 1999–2004

◄ Seglarträff im Hafen
  Seglarträff in the harbour

Seglarträff
Seglarträff

◀ Seeräuber an Land
  Pirates ashore

Nautineum auf dem Dänholm, Unterwasserlabor Helgoland
Nautineum nautical museum on Dänholm island:
the Helgoland Underwater Laboratory

Nautineum, Schifffahrtszeichen ➤
Nautineum museum: navigation buoys

Gotische Ausmalungen in Arkadenzwickeln des Hohen Chores von St. Nikolai
Gothic paintings on the arcade spandrels of the High Choir in St. Nicholas'

◄ Die astronomische Uhr in St. Nikolai (1394)
The astronomical clock of St. Nicholas' Church (1394)

Nautineum und Marinemuseum
Nautineum and Naval Museum

Wintertag
Winter's day

◄ **Marienkirche**
St. Mary's Church

263

Einkaufscenter »Strelapark« am Grünhufer Bogen
Strelapark shopping centre in Grünhufer Bogen Street

Marienkrönungsaltar
Altar of the Coronation of the Virgin Mary

◄ St. Marien
  St. Mary's

Vertrag von 1316 mit mittelalterlichen Siegeln
Contract of 1316 with medieval seals

Pietà von Ernst Barlach im Johanniskloster ➤
Pietà by Ernst Barlach in St. John's Monastery

Trelleborger Platz
Trelleborger Square

◄ Pelikane am Leo-Tolstoi-Weg
Pelicans on Leo Tolstoy Way

277

Frühling: Knieper Nord
Spring: Knieper North district

◄ Prohner Straße
Prohner Strasse

»Regenbogen mit dem Häwelmann« im Stadtteil Knieper West
'Rainbow with the Häwelmann' in Knieper West

Christmas spirit in Ossenreyerstrasse | 287

Pferde im Zoo
Horses in the zoo

◄ Erdholländermühle aus dem 18. Jh. an neuem Standort, dem Zoo
The C18th Erdholländer mill in its new location in the zoo

290 | Der Tribseer Damm mit dem Bahnhof von 1905

Freizeitpark »Hansedom« am Grünhufer Bogen
The Hansedom Leisure park in Grünhufer Bogen Street

296 | St. Nikolai und Rathaus in festlicher Beleuchtung

St. Nicholas' and the City Hall in festive lighting | 297

Kreisverkehr an der Werftkreuzung
Roundabout near the shipyard

Bürgermeister L.-Steinwich-Denkmal von W. Jacobi am Wulflamufer ▶
Mayor L. Steinwich Memorial by W. Jacobi on Wulflamufer Street

300 | Die neue Rügenbrücke – größte Schrägseilbrücke Deutschlands, 2007

The new Rügen Bridge – largest cable-stayed bridge in Germany, 2007 |

Das Theater am Olof-Palme-Platz
The theatre at Olof Palme Square

Wallensteintage
Wallenstein Festival

The Landsknechts (mercenaries) on the Old Market

Riesenrad auf dem Weihnachtsmarkt
Ferris wheel at the Christmas Market

Stralsund-Lichter ➤
Lights of Stralsund

310 | Der Knieperteich im Winter

The Knieper Pond in winter | 311

Weitere Titel dieser Reihe

Impressum

Die Deutsche Nationalbibliothek verzeichnet diese Publikation
in der Deutschen Nationalbibliografie;
detaillierte bibliografische Daten sind im Internet über
http://dnb.d-nb.de abrufbar.

1. Auflage 2018
© Steffen Verlag GmbH, Berliner Allee 38, 13088 Berlin, Tel. (030) 41 93 50 14
info@steffen-verlag.de, www.steffen-verlag.de

Alle Rechte für die Fotos liegen beim Fotografen Harry Hardenberg, Stralsund.

Herstellung: STEFFEN MEDIA, Friedland – Berlin – Usedom, www.steffen-media.de

ISBN 978-3-95799-055-6